This coloring book provides illustrations to go along with the libretto for Handel's *Messiah*. The words to an opera or oratorio are called its *libretto,* whereas, in a stage play, the words are called the *script,* and in a movie they're called the *screenplay.*

Libretto means "little book" in Italian, and that's precisely what it is, because singing a sentence takes about three times longer than saying it. This creates a full evening in the theater or concert hall. The libretto has a huge impact on its music. The words influence the rhythm and melody of a musical phrase. The emotion in the story affects the mood of the music, and the plot determines the overall structure of the opera or oratorio.

An oratorio differs from an opera in that it is a large musical composition for orchestra, choir, and soloists as a concert rather than a theatrical production. Handel's *Messiah* is considered a sacred oratorio because it deals with a sacred topic, Jesus the Messiah, taken from the teachings of the Bible. The words to *Messiah* are a Scripture selection by Charles Jennens from the King James Bible and the Book of Common Prayer. They are modified for the music.

Handel began composing *Messiah* on August 22, 1741. He completed the arrangement in twenty-four days of breathtaking intensity. The first performance of *Messiah* was in Dublin in 1742. It has been in continuous performance for over 250 years.

The conductor directing the musical performance chooses the version or edition of Handel's *Messiah* which will be performed. If you are following along with a concert, you may find a slight variation in the libretto of the performance from the libretto in the coloring book.

Selections from the King James Bible and the Book of Common in this coloring book are public domain.

Illustrations for the *Messiah* Coloring Book
created by Taylor Leong
© 2016
ISBN-13: 978-1536932812
ISBN-10: 1536932817

All rights reserved. No portion of this book may be reproduced, stored in a retrieval system, or transmitted in any form or by any means – electronic, mechanical, photocopy, recording, scanning, or other – without the prior written permission of the artist.

Comfort ye, comfort ye My people, saith your God.
Speak ye comfortably to Jerusalem,
and cry unto her, that her warfare is accomplished,
that her iniquity is pardoned.
The voice of him that crieth in the wilderness;
prepare ye the way of the Lord;
make straight in the desert a highway for our God.
(Isaiah 40:1-3)

Ev'ry valley shall be exalted,
and ev'ry mountain and hill made low;
the crooked straight and the rough places plain.
(Isaiah 40:4)

And the glory of the Lord shall be revealed,
and all flesh shall see it together:
for the mouth of the Lord hath spoken it.
(Isaiah 40:5)

Thus saith the Lord, the Lord of Hosts:
Yet once a little while and I will shake the heavens and the earth,
the sea and the dry land.
And I will shake all nations;
and the desire of all nations shall come.
(Haggai 2:6-7)

The Lord, whom ye seek, shall suddenly come to His temple,
even the messenger of the Covenant, whom ye delight in;
behold, He shall come, saith the Lord of Hosts.
(Malachi 3:1)

**But who may abide the day of His coming,
and who shall stand when He appeareth?
For He is like a refiner's fire.
(Malachi 3:2)**

**And He shall purify the sons of Levi,
that they may offer unto the Lord
an offering in righteousness.
(Malachi 3:3)**

**Behold, a virgin shall conceive and bear a Son,
and shall call His name Emmanuel, God with us.
(Isaiah 7:14; Matthew 1:23)**

**O thou that tellest good tidings to Zion,
get thee up into the high mountain.
O thou that tellest good tidings to Jerusalem,
lift up thy voice with strength; lift it up, be not afraid;
say unto the cities of Judah, behold your God!
(Isaiah 40:9)**

**Arise, shine, for thy Light is come,
and the glory of the Lord is risen upon thee.
(Isaiah 60:1)**

**For behold, darkness shall cover the earth,
and gross darkness the people;
but the Lord shall arise upon thee,
and His glory shall be seen upon thee,
And the Gentiles shall come to thy light,
and kings to the brightness of thy rising.
(Isaiah 60:2-3)**

**The people that walked in darkness have seen a great light;
and they that dwell in the land of the shadow of death,
upon them hath the light shined.
(Isaiah 9:2)**

**For unto us a Child is born, unto us a Son is given,
and the government shall be upon His shoulder;
and His name shall be called,
Wonderful, Counsellor, the Mighty God,
the Everlasting Father, the Prince of Peace.
(Isaiah 9:6)**

**There were shepherds abiding in the field,
keeping watch over their flock by night.
(Luke 2:8)**

**And lo, the angel of the Lord came upon them, and
the glory of the Lord shone round about them, and
they were sore afraid.
(Luke 2:9)**

**And the angel said unto them, Fear not: for behold,
I bring you good tidings of great joy, which shall be to all people.
For unto you is born this day in the City of David a Saviour,
which is Christ the Lord.
(Luke 2:10-11)**

**And suddenly there was with the angel a multitude of the heav'nly host,
praising God, and saying Glory to God in the highest,
and peace on earth, goodwill towards men.
(Luke 2:13-14)**

**Rejoice greatly, O daughter of Zion, shout,
O daughter of Jerusalem:
behold, thy King cometh unto thee:
He is the righteous Saviour,
and He shall speak peace unto the heathen.
(Zechariah 9:9-10)**

**Then shall the eyes of the blind be open'd,
and the ears of the deaf unstopped; then
shall the lame man leap as an hart, and
the tongue of the dumb shall sing.
(Isaiah 35:5-6)**

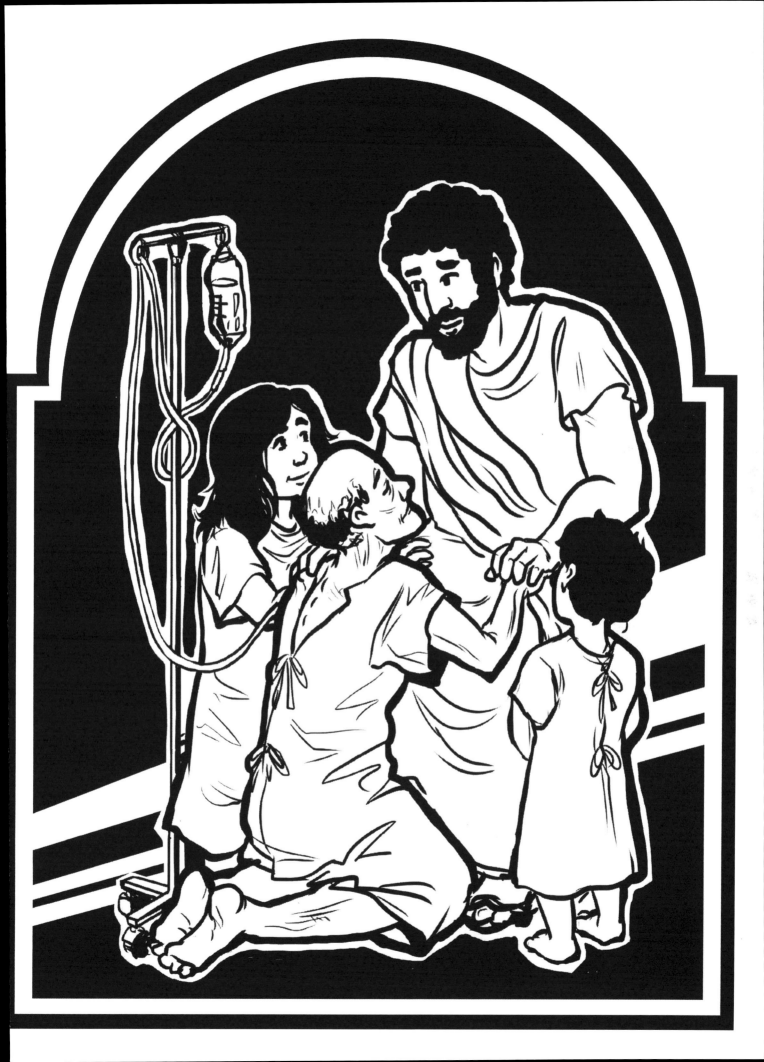

**He shall feed His flock like a shepherd, and
He shall gather the lambs with His arm; and
carry them in His bosom,
and gently lead those that are with young.
Come unto Him all ye that labour,
come unto Him that are heavy laden,
and He will give you rest.
Take His yoke upon you, and learn of Him,
for He is meek and lowly of heart,
and ye shall find rest unto your souls.
(Isaiah 40:11; Matthew 11:28-29)**

**His yoke is easy, and His burden is light.
(Matthew 11:30)**

Behold the Lamb of God,
that taketh away the sin of the world.
(John 1:29)

He was despised and rejected of men,
a man of sorrows and acquainted with grief.
(Isaiah 53:3)

He gave His back to the smiters,
and His cheeks to them that plucked off the hair:
He hid not His face from shame and spitting.
(Isaiah 50:6)

Surely He hath borne our griefs, and carried our sorrows!
He was wounded for our transgressions,
He was bruised for our iniquities;
the chastisement of our peace was upon Him.
(Isaiah 53:4-5)

And with His stripes we are healed.
(Isaiah 53:5)

All we like sheep have gone astray;
we have turned every one to his own way.
And the Lord hath laid on Him the iniquity of us all.
(Isaiah 53:6)

All they that see Him laugh Him to scorn;
they shoot out their lips, and shake their heads, saying:
(Psalm 22:7)

He trusted in God that He would deliver Him;
let Him deliver Him, if He delight in Him.
(Psalm 22:8)

**Thy rebuke hath broken His heart:
He is full of heaviness.
He looked for some to have pity on Him,
but there was no man,
neither found He any to comfort Him.
(Psalm 69:20)**

**Behold, and see if there be any sorrow
like unto His sorrow.
(Lamentations 1:12)**

**He was cut off out of the land of the living:
for the transgressions of Thy people was He stricken.
(Isaiah 53:8)**

**But Thou didst not leave His soul in hell;
nor didst Thou suffer Thy Holy One to see corruption.
(Psalm 16:10)**

**Lift up your heads, O ye gates; and be ye lift up,
ye everlasting doors;
and the King of Glory shall come in.**

**Who is this King of Glory?
The Lord strong and mighty,
the Lord mighty in battle,**

**Lift up your heads, O ye gates; and be lift up,
ye everlasting doors;
and the King of Glory shall come in.**

**Who is this King of Glory?
The Lord of Hosts, He is the King of Glory.
(Psalm 24:7-10)**

**Unto which of the angels said
He at any time:
Thou art My Son,
this day have I begotten Thee?
(Hebrews 1:5)**

**Let all the angels of God worship Him.
(Hebrews 1:6)**

**Thou art gone up on high;
Thou hast led captivity captive,
and received gifts for men;
yea, even from Thine enemies,
that the Lord God might dwell among them.
(Psalm 68:18)**

The Lord gave the word;
great was the company of the preachers.
(Psalm 68:11)

How beautiful are the feet of them
that preach the gospel of peace, and
bring glad tidings of good things.
(Isaiah 52:7; Romans 10:15)

Their sound is gone out into all lands, and
their words unto the ends of the world.
(Romans 10:18; Psalm 19:4)

Why do the nations so furiously rage together,
and why do the people imagine a vain thing?
The kings of the earth rise up,
and the rulers take counsel together against the Lord,
and against His Anointed.
(Psalm 2:1-2)

Let us break their bonds asunder,
and cast away their yokes from us.
(Psalm 2:3)

He that dwelleth in heaven shall laugh them to scorn;
the Lord shall have them in derision.
(Psalm 2:4)

Thou shalt break them with a rod of iron;
thou shalt dash them in pieces like a potter's vessel.
(Psalm 2:9)

Hallelujah: for the Lord God Omnipotent reigneth.
(Revelation 19:6)

The kingdom of this world is become the kingdom of our Lord,
and of His Christ;
and He shall reign for ever and ever.
(Revelation 11:15)

King of Kings, and Lord of Lords.
(Revelation 19:16)

I know that my Redeemer liveth,
and that he shall stand at the latter day upon the earth.
And though worms destroy this body,
yet in my flesh shall I see God.
(Job 19:25-26)

For now is Christ risen from the dead,
the first fruits of them that sleep.
(1Corinthians 15:20)

Since by man came death,
by man came also the resurrection of the dead.
For as in Adam all die,
even so in Christ shall all be made alive.
(1Corinthians 15:21-22)

Behold, I tell you a mystery; we shall not all sleep,
but we shall all be changed in a moment,
in the twinkling of an eye, at the last trumpet.
(1Corinthinas 15:51-52)

The trumpet shall sound,
and the dead shall be raised incorruptible,
and we shall be changed.
For this corruptible must put on incorruption
and this mortal must put on immortality.
(1Corinthians 15:52-53)

Then shall be brought to pass the saying that is written:
Death is swallowed up in victory.
(1Corinthians 15:54)

O death, where is thy sting?
O grave, where is thy victory?
The sting of death is sin, and the strength of sin is the law.
(1Corinthians 15:55-56)

But thanks be to God, who giveth us the victory
through our Lord Jesus Christ.
(1Corinthians 15:57)

If God is for us, who can be against us?
(Romans 8:31)

Who shall lay anything to the charge of God's elect?
It is God that justifieth, who is he that condemneth?
It is Christ that died, yea rather, that is risen again,
who is at the right hand of God, who makes intercession for us.
(Romans 8:33-34)

**Worthy is the Lamb that was slain,
and hath redeemed us to God by His blood,
to receive power, and riches, and wisdom,
and strength, and honour, and glory, and blessing.
Blessing and honour, glory and power, be unto Him
that sitteth upon the throne, and unto the Lamb,
for ever and ever.
Amen.
(Revelation 5:12-14)**